Why Do My Teeth Fall Out?

And Other Questions Kids Have About the Human Body

by Heather L. Montgomery   illustrated by Jon Davis

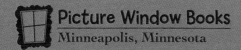

Picture Window Books

Minneapolis, Minnesota

Acknowledgments
This book was produced for Picture Window Books
by Bender Richardson White, U.K.

Illustrations by Jon Davis
Consultant: John Stidworthy, Scientific Fellow of the Zoological Society,
London, and former Lecturer in the Education Department,
Natural History Museum, London

Picture Window Books
A Capstone Imprint
151 Good Counsel Drive
P.O. Box 669
Mankato, MN 56002-0669
877-845-8392
www.capstonepub.com

 All books published by Picture Window Books are manufactured
with paper containing at least 10 percent post-consumer waste.

Library of Congress Cataloging-in-Publication Data
Montgomery, Heather L.
Why do my teeth fall out? : and other questions kids have about the
human body / by Heather L. Montgomery ; illustrated by Jon Davis.
p. cm. — (Kids' questions)
Includes index.
ISBN 978-1-4048-5530-4 (library binding)
ISBN 978-1-4048-6534-1 (paperback)
1. Human body—Juvenile literature. I. Davis, Jon. II. Title.
QP37.M693 2010
612.4'63—dc22   2009017863

Printed in the United States of America in North Mankato, Minnesota.
042011   006178R

HUMAN BODY

Kids have lots of questions about their bodies. What is my body made of? How do my muscles move my bones? What happens when I swallow food? How do my heart, eyes, and brain work? In this book, kids get answers.

How many bones do I have in my body?

Hollister, age 7

When you were born, you had 300 bones. By the time you are an adult, you will have only 206! Some of the bones join together as you grow.

Why do I have to have bones?

Mia, age 8

Your bones are like tent poles. They hold your body up. If you didn't have bones, you would fall down. Bones help protect organs such as your brain and heart. Also, bones work with your muscles to help you move.

How can my body move?

Javier, age 8

Muscles and bones work together to help your body move. Each end of a muscle is connected to a different bone. When you tighten a muscle, it shortens and pulls one bone toward the other.

BICEPS MUSCLE PULLING UP THE ARM

How do I get growing pains?

Keara, age 7

No one knows how you get growing pains. It is a mystery of science. Usually you can make yourself feel better by rubbing your muscles or stretching your arms and legs.

How does my brain work?

Aaron, age 8

Your brain controls your body. For example, if your eyes see something dangerous, they send a message to your brain. Your brain decides that you need to move away. It then sends a message to your leg muscles to move your body! Your brain also tells you other things, such as when to go to the bathroom. It tells your heart to beat and your lungs to breathe. And it helps you learn.

Why don't I think the same as other people?

Hunter, age 8

Your brain stores information that you have learned, such as how to play soccer. When you think, you use your stored information. Because no two people have exactly the same experiences, your brain holds information that is different from anyone else's. That's why you can think differently.

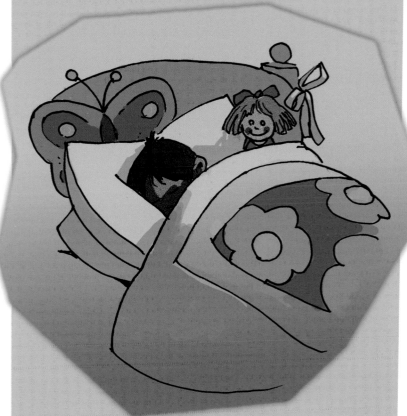

How can I sleep?

Samantha, age 8

At night, your brain tells your body to sleep. You close your eyes. Your heart slows down. Your muscles relax. You need sleep to rest, heal, and grow. Your brain needs time to sort what it learned during the day.

7

How do my feet fall asleep?

Madison, age 8

Nerves carry messages between your body and your brain. If you sit on your leg, you might squash the nerves connected to your foot. The messages get mixed-up, and you feel pins and needles.

How do my eyes know when to blink?

Kindergartners

How do reflexes work?

2nd graders

When something comes too close to your eyes, nerves carry messages from them to your spine. The messages come back quickly to tell your eyelids to close. This happens without you even thinking. It is automatic. All reflexes work like that. Sneezing is a reflex, too.

How good do my ears hear?

Bereket, age 6

Some animals, including people, have better hearing than others. For example, most people can hear better than most birds, but not as well as a cat. Your ears catch sound waves out of the air. Their cup shape makes catching sounds easier.

How do my eyes work?

Arianna, age 3

You see things when light bounces off objects, such as a toy. The light enters the black part of your eye, called the pupil. At first, the image is upside-down. But then the light turns on nerves at the back of your eye. Those nerves carry messages to your brain. Your brain turns the image the right way, and you see the toy.

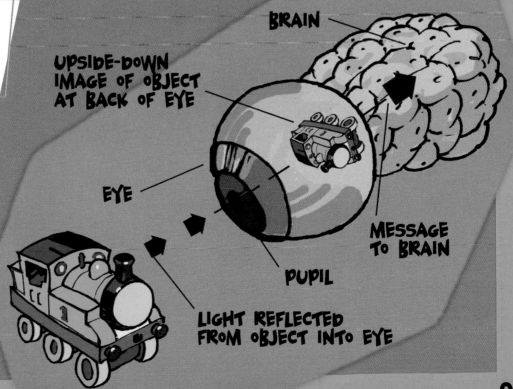

BRAIN

UPSIDE-DOWN IMAGE OF OBJECT AT BACK OF EYE

EYE

MESSAGE TO BRAIN

PUPIL

LIGHT REFLECTED FROM OBJECT INTO EYE

How does my heart pump blood?

Josie, age 8

Do I have blood in my whole body?

Gavin, age 6

The muscles in your heart squeeze. That pushes blood through tubes called blood vessels. The vessels carry blood from your heart to your lungs and then to every part of your body.

How much blood do I have in my body?

Abigale, age 8

Your body holds almost 1 gallon (3.8 liters) of blood.

How big is my heart?

Arianna, age 3

Your heart is about the size of your fist. It is shaped like an upside-down pear.

How many times does my heart beat in one day?

Hannah, age 7

Does my heart ever get tired?

Dillon, age 7

Your heart beats about 90 times every minute. That is about 129,600 beats per day. And it never gets tired!

How long can a human run without stopping?

Antonio, age 8

One man ran for more than three days! He ran 350 miles (560 kilometers) without stopping. Some people need a break after 100 yards (91 meters). Others can run marathons—more than 26 miles (42 km). With training, most people can build up their running strength and distances.

How do my lungs work?

Elaina, age 8

When you breathe, you pull air into your lungs. In your lungs, your blood trades gases with the air. Your blood gets oxygen and gets rid of waste gas. When you hold your breath, the lungs don't get any fresh air. They sense this and tell your body to breathe!

What do I use to sing?
Ismail, age 7

How can I talk?
Ismail, age 7

You use your lungs, throat, and mouth to sing and talk. Your lungs push air over two vocal cords in your throat. The cords shake back and forth quickly. This makes a sound. You use your tongue and lips to change the sound into words.

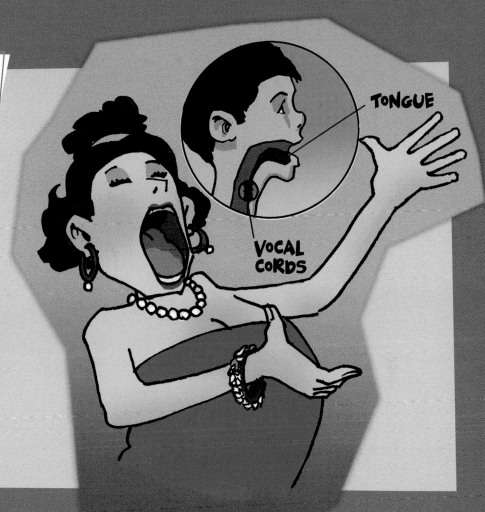

How do tonsils help my throat?
Paul, age 8

Tonsils catch germs from the air you breathe. They help get rid of the germs so you do not get sick.

13

How does water go down my throat and end up in the right pipe?

Ben, age 6

Your throat has two tubes. One goes to your lungs. The other goes to your stomach. When you swallow, a flap closes off the tube to your lungs so water and food can go down the right tube.

Why do my teeth fall out?

Jordan, age 8

How do my teeth get loose?

Kindergartners

Baby teeth are too small for a grown-up mouth. Grown-up teeth push through your gums, making your baby teeth fall out.

14

How does my belly really work?
Alex, age 6

How do I go to the bathroom?
Nate, age 8

In your belly, muscles and stomach juices break down food into tiny pieces. Your blood takes in the food bits. The parts that cannot be used by your body are passed down a tube to your bottom. When you go to the bathroom, you squeeze that tube to get rid of the waste.

How can I chew and get it down my throat?
Ben, age 6

Chewing breaks food into small pieces. Your tongue and muscles push the pieces down your throat, toward your stomach.

How does milk help me get strong?

Owen, age 5

You eat food and drink liquids to get nutrients your body needs. Milk has lots of calcium. Your bones need calcium to be solid and strong. Your muscles need calcium to move.

Why is an apple healthy, and does it really keep the doctor away?

Zarah, age 5

Apples and other kinds of fruit have nutrients that may block some diseases. Eating lots of fruits and vegetables may help to keep you healthy so you do not have to go to the doctor.

What is my body made of?

Christine, age 7

How much water does my body need?

Emily, age 7

Your body is mostly water. The amount you need depends on what you are doing. When you run and jump, your body uses more water than when you sit quietly. When it's hot outside, you need more water. Your body has a special way of telling you that you need water—you feel thirsty!

How many colors can people be?

Hunter, age 8

People can be one of many colors, ranging from light to dark. In your skin are tiny pieces of color, called pigment. The darker you are, the more pigment you have. Like sunscreen, pigment helps block light from hurting your skin.

Why do I have freckles?

Christine, age 7

Pigment in your skin can clump together. That makes a freckle. If your parents have freckles, you may have them, too.

How does my hair grow?

Dawson, age 8

How do fingernails grow?

Giselle, age 8

New hair and fingernail parts push up from roots under your skin. The parts you see are no longer living. That's why it doesn't hurt to cut them.

Why do I sweat so bad?

Samantha, age 8

Your body sweats to cool off. If you get too hot, you will get sick.

How was I born?

Anna, age 4

A baby grows inside a woman for about nine months. When the baby is big enough, the woman gives birth. The baby is born!

Does a baby have a hole in its head?

Larry, age 7

A baby has gaps between the bones in its head. The gaps make parts of the skull soft. This makes it easier for the mother to give birth. Later, the bones grow together.

Why are some people small and some people are tall?
Luis, age 8

How tall can people grow?
Michael, age 7

Most adults are around 5 feet 8 inches (173 centimeters) tall. The tallest person ever was 8 feet 11 inches (272 cm). The smallest was only 24 inches (61 cm). People inherit their height from their parents. If your parents are tall, you are likely to be tall, too.

Why do kids grow but grown-ups don't?
Aiden, age 5

When do I stop growing?
Josie, age 8

Your brain sends signals to your body to tell it to keep growing. When you are about 18 years old, your brain quits sending the signals, so you stop growing.

How come we all have to die?

Zarah, age 5

How long can I live?

Josie, age 8

People are animals. All animals are born, they live, and then they die. This life cycle makes room on the planet for other animals. Healthy people often live more than 75 years. One woman in France lived 122 years!

Why do you not have eyeballs when you're a skeleton?

Mia, age 8

After a body dies, it begins to rot. The soft parts, such as the eyes, stomach, and muscles, go first. The hard bones of the skeleton last longer.

TO LEARN MORE

More Books to Read

Levine, Shar, and Leslie Johnstone. *The Amazing Human Body.* New York: Sterling Pub., 2006.

Robinson, Richard. *The Human Body.* Laguna Hills, Calif.: QEB Pub., 2007.

Seuling, Barbara. *You Blink Twelve Times a Minute: and Other Freaky Facts About the Human Body.* Minneapolis: Picture Window Books, 2009.

Simon, Seymour. *The Human Body.* New York: HarperCollins Children's Books, 2008.

Internet Sites

FactHound offers a safe, fun way to find Internet sites related to this book. All of the sites have been researched by our staff.

Here's all you do:

Visit *www.facthound.com*

FactHound will fetch the best sites for you!

GLOSSARY

blood vessels—tubes that carry blood through your body

calcium—a nutrient found in milk and used by your bones and muscles

germs—very small living things that can make you sick

inherit—to receive features from your parents

intestines—long tubes below your stomach that digest food

nerve—a thin fiber that carries messages between your body and your brain

nutrient—something your body needs to grow and stay healthy

oxygen—a gas in the air that animals and humans need to survive

pigment—a substance that gives color

reflex—an automatic reaction of your body

skeleton—the framework of bones that support and protect your body

vocal cord—a thin flap, or membrane, in your throat that makes sounds

INDEX

Look for all of the titles in the Kids' Questions series:

Did Dinosaurs Eat People? And Other Questions Kids Have About Dinosaurs
What Is the Moon Made Of? And Other Questions Kids Have About Space
What's Inside a Rattlesnake's Rattle? And Other Questions Kids Have About Snakes
Why Do My Teeth Fall Out? And Other Questions Kids Have About the Human Body